To my Friend Colleen

Thank you so much for
your support and I
appreciate everything that
you do.

Monae

THE
GLORIOUS
Magnificent
PRESENCE

Special Limited Edition

FIRST EDITION

The Glorious Magnificent Presence

By Monad Elohim Graves

TABLE OF CONTENTS

Acknowledgment

I WOULD LIKE TO DEDICATE THIS BOOK TO
ALL OF MY FRIENDS WHO HAVE RESPECTED
AND LOVED ME FOR WHO I AM.

I would also like to thank everyone who has
encouraged me to continue on my journey and the
quest to be the best that I can be in this life.

I am thankful for all of my family, friends, and
acquaintances and I want you to know that your
presence; even though It was only a momentary
second in the scheme of things, was a wonderfully
inspiring experience for me.

**To everyone who has supported and believed in
me.**
I want you to know that you made my life so much
worth living, and I will always treasure every
second, minute, hour, and day of the loving and
peaceful energy vibrations that we shared. **To
everyone who passed through my life,** I am truly
honored that you shared the presence of the beauty
of your spirit with me and know that we are all one
in spirit always.

Foreword

D ear reader in writing this book there are chapters which have photos of some of the many original one-of-a-kind sculptures that I have created. These photos reflect and symbolize different stages of my life and my consciousness development and are pictorial representations of my progress along the way of self-awareness and how to attain and maintain, love, peace, hope, and joy in my life and mind! Even though the photos of some of my artistic creations are not entirely exact representations or may appear to not accurately reflect the nature of the subjects that I am writing about, they are true symbols which are a direct result which reflect my effort to be the best that I can be. They are also a result of me making a constant effort to use self-discipline in my daily thought, emotional and physical life practices. I hope that when you read my book you will understand and enjoy my effort to share with you some of the essences of the quality of my over standing and understanding as a result of my lifelong journey into the mystery, consciousness and awareness of the **Magnificent Glorious Presence** which dwells within and without the scene of all beings.

Respectfully Yours,
Monad Elohim Graves

Introduction

Dear reader,
I am hopeful that as a result of you reading this book, you will tap into the flow of my

ideas, wisdom, knowledge, and understanding about life, the people, animals, and the things in life.

To not only broaden your awareness of the reality of who you are in this body but also to help escort and guide you through the process of thought and understanding, which may expand your comprehension and awareness of self, and also open your eyes and mind to the reality of the one life which dwells in all, revealing to you the truth of who you are and enlightening you to who you are in relation to others.

This book aims to unravel the mystery of the identity of the one life shared by all in this human, unconscious, mental dream world unreality.

Join me on my journey of inner mind exploration, which will transport you beyond the boundaries of thought into another level of consciousness thought reality. A reality that will reveal and open doors of other realms of wonderous and joyous possibilities, awakening you to the perception, revelation, and consciousness of your infinite, radiant, divine self.

You may ask yourself, why am I reading this book? Because it is time for you to hear the message in this book, a testimonial that extends beyond the herd mentality of the masses who have been conditioned to a lifetime of mental and emotional slavery. Imprisoned within the cycle of the endless pursuit of temporary enjoyments of the flesh, that will oftentimes leave a person unsatisfied and thirsting for feelings of a lasting peace and joy, only found through the searching of one's soul.

Of course, many people may need more time to consider what I am suggesting in this book; I am aware that there are many paths that will eventually reach the goal of self-discovery.

With great enthusiasm and joy, I am delighted and honored to share with you, through the writing of this book, the results of my voyage of a lifetime, exploring my soul and seeking the mysteries of life in this temporary, momentary, dream world reality. This book is documented proof and record of my uninterrupted, determined pursuit to discover the hidden self within.

When you read my words and glean some understanding from my interpretations and direct contact with the spirit, it may illuminate and allow you to penetrate to the essence of the knowledge and wisdom I am sharing with you, to help and perhaps better assist you in creating a position and a reference point in your heart and mind, to see the truth in my words and the illuminating expansive vision that extends beyond the babble of the mind, focusing your gaze, and gaining an intuitive insight, to strengthen your mental power, increase your comprehension to penetrate through the wall of illusion, and once accomplished, reveal the actual reality perceived from the soul's perspective.

As you explore the knowledge and wisdom in this book, you will gradually part the veil of the mind's ignorance and denial about the person experiencing this life. You will once again bask in the radiance of the wisdom of the soul's light and illuminating power of the divine presence within all life forms, in our present dream world reality.

By reading this book in your present stage of physical, mental, and emotional development, I know that you will connect with the rhythm and cadence of my words; words that will assist, help, and guide you along the path of understanding with me, as we start this journey of soul exploration. I ask you; Are you ready to join me on this journey? Are you prepared to proceed with me as we explore this ancient path? A path that takes us beyond the endless chatter of the mind's mental imaginings as it gropes in the dark passageways and maze of endless possibilities of the mind's ignorance.

Come with me as we observe how the mind interprets life's realities through preoccupations, investigations, and endless inquiries about the nature of the temporary forms in our thought dream world reality, which has always existed in the inner sanctuary of the mind lest traveled only by souls yearning to be free. Free from the illusion of the misguided perception of the separation of forms in the illusion of our thought dream world reality.

As we proceed on our journey, we will break down the barriers and walls of previous mental conditioning, which creates an impediment that often blocks our comprehension of the reality hidden behind the appearance of forms, hindering and blinding us as we try to go beyond the realm of the minds imaginings, as it tries to formulate and interpret our illusionary thought world experience. A world we perceive as accurate, but in reality, is only composed of the forms and misinterpretations of the illusions of thought.

We have been conditioned to see life narrowly, and the thoughts and ideas that support this way of interpreting reality have crystalized and prevented us from seeing life as it is. These handed-down illusionary thoughts of previous misconceptions about life have been shared from generations to the present. We have been programmed and conditioned to think, see, and feel that the forms we perceive in our daily reality are factual.

This has fostered a misperception that hinders us from understanding and comprehending the nature of the mind's creative energy.

As you prepare to take this excursion with me, let my words and the ideas that this book contain propel you to a greater understanding, transporting you beyond any misunderstanding, or lack of comprehension, of the uncommon knowledge and wisdom and reality of what I will be revealing in this books message. The only thing that is required for you to understand, substantiate, and gain a clear understanding of what I am sharing, is to open up your heart and mind without prejudging before you read the chapters in this book. Have an open mind!

I hope that as you direct your attention and focus the light of your mind upon my words, it will kindle the interest of your higher self, penetrating through any personal character bias or judgments that may prevent you from reading this book with an open heart and a curious expansive mind.

If you succeed in this challenge, it will feed, nourish, and awaken your soul, giving life to your spirit with the power of love burning deep within my heart. I encourage you to listen with your heart, and if you do so, you will gradually begin to see, hear, and feel the message that I am sharing from my soul directly to your soul.

As you read my words, may your soul capture the melody of the musical vibration and rhythm of my words which will help dissolve any fog or misunderstanding you may have in your mind as you read this book.

Many years ago, I undertook a voyage and adventure along an ancient path of knowledge and understanding. This ancient path has always existed within the inner chambers of our mind, waiting to transport us beyond the boundaries of the mind's mental imaginings. By walking this path, I have been significantly rewarded, and this journey has revealed to me the truth of our existence.

This thirst and desire for knowledge has enlightened me greatly and I have become more aware of the reality of the world of things, scenes, and beings; and how; by me paying attention to how I think in the world, and also by me paying attention to my thoughts, and mindfully taking control of what I choose to think, say, and do in my daily life experience.

Coming into the awareness of these essential thought practices has also helped me to shape my daily life's reality productively; this method of thinking has helped me to create a mindset within my mind that promotes love and peace in the world, using love as an transmissible quality medium, which helps me to do everything in my power to demonstrate through practice, how to make the world a better place to live; making love the light of my life's purpose, as well as practicing love in all of my life's trials and tribulations.

Through trial and error, I learned the value of applying love in all my associations and encounters in my life's everyday thought occurrences, because love is the most extraordinary power in the world that if applied in thoughts and actions, will eventually remove the veil of ignorance from our eyes, to reveal the true identity of the divine presence, within all forms.

By making these sacrifices in my life, it has been revealed to me the importance of seeking self-mastery, and also making a serious effort to tame the various forms of my nature, such as dietary practices, developing some level of control of my thought habits, taming and regulating the beast of feelings, wants, and desires. Why; because thoughts are things, and whatever a person thinks in this world will eventually come true, especially if used with the power of the imagination.

Through practice, consistency, and sustaining a daily life of self-discipline, paying attention to what I allow myself to think, and becoming conscious and aware of how I relate to people in the world. This thought discipline has revealed to me how thoughts materialize into vibrations, vibrations into energy, and energy into the illusionary forms that we witness in our present dream reality.

Oh, what an incredibly magical and mystical journey I have undertaken; to pay attention to what I will allow myself to think in the world, being mindful and consciously thinking loving thoughts has compelled and propelled me forward and also captivated and mesmerized me by the power and the incredible radiating influence of the force of the soul; an incomprehensible, force of vibrational thought energy,

This energy has been an immeasurable, unique gift, and a helpful and practical guide for me as I travel through this life and has also left me captivated and in complete awe of the glorious radiance of the divine presence. A presence that is the main point in my consciousness, and like a burning flame, has seared my heart with feelings of peace and joy from realizing the wisdom of the power of the Glorious Magnificent Presence. The presence that has changed my life for the better, forever.

This book is documented proof and a record of my endless and untiring pursuit to discover the hidden self within.

This quest and adventure that I undertook years ago to find the truth of our existence has rewarded me immensely and has allowed me to become more aware of the reality of other worlds, things, scenes, and beings, and how; by me paying attention to how I think in the world, realizing the value of making a daily effort to; skillfully and mindfully develop the habit of watching my thoughts and what I think, say, and do in my everyday life experience, and also making love the light of my life, as well as practicing love in all of my daily trials and tribulations.

Through trial and error, I learned the value of applying love in all of my associations and encounters with others in my life's daily thought occurrences because thoughts are things, and thoughts materialize into the scenes of life on this imaginary material plane of existence.

Chapter One

Who Are You?

When you look into the mirror and see an image of your body which is just a reflection of your body. But Is it you?

Come and take a journey with me as we examine the image of your body in the mirror of your mind, to progress forward and go beyond the fog of the minds speculations, misunderstandings, and misinterpretations about the nature of actual reality in our short temporary life existence, in the world of form in this dream reality experience. Come with me as I share with you the results of my journey along the ancient road of consciousness awareness, illuminated by the soul's light, to reveal the reality of who you are and, most importantly, who you are in relations to others.

As you read my words, they will open up vast realms of wonderous possibilities that will perhaps expand your understanding of the nature of thought and its relationship to our life in the perceived physical world. I would like to assist you to increase your knowledge and feasibly be an aid to help guide you across the gulf of ignorance between what is traditionally taught and considered to be accurate into greater levels of expansive possibilities.

Possibilities, if comprehended and rings true for you, will open you up to a different perspective of life in the world beyond the typical, widespread knowledge that we have been taught about the world in this temporary stage of unconsciousness and misunderstanding of life. As we investigate and inquire to find the solutions to our quest, we will grow more aware of bathing in the light, vibration, and energy of the omni- present divine radiant presence. The magic and miracle of this effort to know ourselves will enhance and awaken us to how we interpret and comprehend our life experiences in our daily waking consciousness. As we proceed, we will be bathing in the glory and power of an awareness that only manifests when we cultivate peace in our hearts and love in our minds.

As you read this book, the message I will share with you will transport and propel you forward into a tremendously expansive knowledge, wisdom, and broader understanding of life which will reveal how life unfolds according to our thoughts. Let us use the power of love as a vehicle to transport us forward on this soul-inspired journey. This journey will take us deeper into other realms of perception, comprehension, and understanding, expanding our awareness beyond our wildest expectations.

Whilst you join me and start down the ancient road of this literary journey, you will establish and awaken the master within you that has always been you, waiting patiently behind the screen and barrier of fog that has been distorting our vision for ages, unimaginable lengths of time that stretches and extends way beyond our present stage of personal mental recollection and ideas about a theoretical concept of the world contained within a so called physical universe, born within the atmosphere and dreams of the minds mental imaginings.

We are no longer conscious of the history of our divine life presence, which is the beginning and ending identity, hidden behind and within all thought manifestations, and all thought forms exhibited within the illusion of the temporary, mental, thought, dream world reality. Our souls are in slumber and we are experiencing misinformation supplied by the minds misunderstanding of truth because it has not been illuminated by the light of consciousness and the awareness of the soul.

Chapter Two

Revealing the Mystery of You

Years ago, as a teaching artist in Washington state, one of my favorite things to do at the beginning of a class session was to tell stories that would help to stimulate thought and increase my student's imagination.

For example, I would start the conversation by asking the students a question. Who are you? When you look into the mirror, what do you see? Whom do you see? Do you see yourself?

I would then ask the question. Do you see your arm? Is your arm you? The students would usually answer No! I would then reply. You are right! Now a day's, doctors can remove your arm, and you will still be able to live, so you are not your arms. Even if you were to lose both of your arms, you could still live with no arms. Suppose you were to lose both arms and legs; did you lose yourself?

No! You can still stay alive with no arms and legs. Suppose you lost your eyes and ears. Can you still live? Yes, you can! You can still live even if you lose both arms, legs, eyes, and ears. What about if you lose the top layer of your skin? Can you still live? Yes, you can! You are not the arms, legs, eyes, ears, or skin.

So, when we look into the mirror, we don't see ourselves, only an image of the outside of our bodies. When we look at our reflection in the mirror, we only see various exterior parts of the body but not the total person, only the surface shell, which is the vehicle we use to function, communicate, and explore in this perceived mental world experience.

Suppose you decide to go for a walk in the morning; who wants to go for a walk in the morning? Your legs don't want to go for a walk in the morning, you want to go for a walk in the morning, and you use your will to move your legs, and they start to walk, taking you wherever you want to go.

When you get hungry and want to eat, does your mouth get hungry? No, your mouth doesn't get hungry; You get hungry, and you use your will to move your mouth to eat your food, and you use your choice to allow your eyes to see the food, and you use your will to move your arms and hands to eat the food.

So who is this invisible you that is getting hungry, and who is this you, this secret life that uses a mouth to chew and gives us the ability to chase all of our fleeting desires and imaginary dreams; who is this ignored, quiet, and subtle presence who is the master and watcher behind all decisions and choices that we make with this body but is ignored because we don't have a sliver of any idea of its eternal presence within us all; because the false sense of the body has blinded us to the awareness of our true self.

Who or what is this invisible force, energy, and life behind the scene that is patiently waiting to reveal itself but hasn't come forward to be recognized in the consciousness of most people because we have been conditioned not to be aware or even curious, of the reality of its presence?

So, let's delve deeper in our search to discover who we are in relation to this Magnificent, Glorious Presence.

We see the outside of the body and realize that it is composed of various parts that make a complete human body, but what about the characteristics and organs of the body that we can't see. Such as the heart, lungs, kidneys, and stomach. Are these parts of the body you? No, but they all work together to keep our bodies operating perfectly throughout our present life experience.

The truth is, none of these things, are you! And their whole purpose is to assist you as you live, and they provide a structure and basic human platform that you can use to learn and grow into a greater awareness in this life, on this world.

You are that hidden life within the body, behind all your wants, needs, aspirations, dreams, thoughts, and desires.

You are the life of the body, and without you, it would fall to the ground in a heap like a bundle of rags.

A good analogy is, like a deep-sea diver who puts on a deep-sea diver's suit to experience life under the water, so do you use a human body to sample life in the air of the days of your present life involvement?

Also, when a deep-sea diver finishes exploring under the water, he comes to the surface and removes the deep-sea diving suit; So, do you remove yourself from your body when you end your discovering and experiencing life in your world.

The life that you are is hidden within the body, and like a puppet master controlling the movements of his puppet, so do you; who is the life behind your body wants, moods, thoughts, hopes, and desires; subjectively control and direct your human body through its life activities, daily trials, errors, and tribulations; directed by you, as it absorbs and learns from your everyday life's experiences faithfully responding to the effortless commands of your indominable will to execute all manner of tasks during your short sojourn in life.

Chapter Three

Parasites the Masters of Cravings

Have you ever noticed that whenever you come to a point in your growth and life to take a step forward, a time in your life when you want to change, and when you make the decision to change your behavior in some way, perhaps for more significant mental or physical health; or maybe you want to lose weight, stop smoking or change and modify your eating habits, from unhealthy to healthier living. And have you ever noticed how difficult it is for us to muster up the willpower to eliminate and change undesirable habits?

We fall short even in situations that sometimes mean the difference between success or failure or life and death. We often cannot succeed because we don't use our willpower to overcome or rise to the occasion to achieve success.

Someday, we will eventually reach a stage in our life where we realize there are things in our lifestyles, habits, and behavior that is holding us back, keeping us from advancing to another level and stage in our growth that we deem necessary for our own, mental, and physical development, and for our self-esteem and satisfaction; a satisfaction that is necessary for our sense of self-worth, and mental wellbeing.

I am not going to sugar coat this subject, I am going to tell it like it is; as far as overcoming the obstacles that we feel may be hindering us from going forward and making progress in achieving our goals are under certain conditions are because of interference; the body is possessed and occupied, all too often by outside spirits and energies. These tiny and mainly hardly ever detected little beings live permanently and are comfortable making their home within us. Most people live their whole life under the influence and suggestions from the consequences of these beings, and the way they make people behave has been considered normal for thousands of years.

Throughout collected humanity's lifetime, these small life forms have disrupted and altered the course and direction of humanity's mental, moral, and spiritual progression, interfering with human's ability to create a paradise on earth. And in one collective human lifetime, they have lived and made their home unnoticed within our bodies, constantly contradicting the natural habits of proper judgment and peaceful conduct necessary for the world to change for the better.

What most people don't realize; and hardly ever consider, is that in many instances, the decisions that are made by humans, seemingly without the thought of the consequences of those decisions or actions, are made; because people are controlled and influenced by outside forces, which have sabotaged, taken possession of, and directed most people's minds from birth. For thousands of years, these foreign influences have been characterized and named the Devil, Satan, Beelzebub, Lucifer, etc. These words were often used to describe hostile hidden forces that influenced people to do evil but in fact are just the effects of our bodies being riddled with thousands of parasites that feed off of our blood and toxic waste from decadent lifestyle practices and unhealthy eating habits, especially eating the flesh of the carcasses of dead animals!

Chapter Four

Fasting

In the past the ancients used fasting to rid the body of these demon/parasites, which the early spiritual practitioners discovered would leave the body when food was withheld for a certain number of days. These lifeforms or parasites and worms have made our bodies their temple. Our bodies have been their church and house of worship since the discovery of fire.

With the discovery of fire, we started cooking our food. By so doing, it also allowed the parasite a door and avenue to gain entry to the inner sanctuary of our body, giving them access to the vulnerabilities inside the tributaries and waters of our system, such as through the arteries of the circulatory, digestion, and lymph systems. They depend on us to cook our food, destroying all of the vitamins and nutrients necessary to keep our bodies and minds healthy. This creates an excellent nesting habitat and home for these intestinal worms.

These foreign invaders, which live within people, are the masters that people serve; we unknowingly obey them by craving unhealthy food and other toxic substances. When we get to the stage of wanting to change our unhealthy habits, we find it difficult, and what we thought were our cravings are the influence of the wants and desires of the worms and parasites which live inside the body temple.

At the heart of most addictions and cravings are parasites inside bodies that need to be cleansed of the accumulation of years of decadent unhealthy eating. As we go throughout our day, we think we are living our life but are unaware of the presence of worms inside us. We are unknowingly living our entire lives to satisfy their impulses, cravings, and desires. In many instances in our daily lives, we think that the thoughts, wants, desires we feel and are our own, not knowing or becoming aware of the fact and reality of how we are possessed and influenced by these parasites who live off of our blood and waste. We think we are making our own decisions. But often, worms are steering the direction of our appetites.

We think that the desires, impulses, and thoughts that we believe are our own but on the contrary, are the wants and needs of the frequency of the passions and cravings of the worms which have taken up lodging in our system.

These cravings and unhealthy influences from the worms in our bodies are the meaning behind the terms such as demons, devils, Satan, Beelzebub, etc. That is why in many cultures, demons were portrayed and described as having two horns and long tails that would make you do evil. Which is an accurate description of the intestinal worms and parasites that live inside our bodies.

The previous paragraph is an excellent definition of how we are controlled by microscopic lifeforms of different shapes and sizes; beings that invade our system through the food we eat and the thoughts we think, and as a result, they are covertly, secretly and cleverly continuously poisoning our blood and interfering with our ability to manifest, peace, love, and harmony with each other In this life.

Let me be clear; Because humans eat food and drink liquids for nourishment, it is impossible to keep away from the multitudes of life forms and parasites in the environment from entering the body through the nose, mouth, ears, and skin. There are many avenues through which they can gain entry into our bodies.

The good thing is that not all parasites are detrimental; some are beneficial to our body's microbiome and help to keep our bodies balanced and healthy. And one of the most powerful tools for regulating a healthy balance of beneficial microbes in our system and ridding the body of all toxins and disease is through periodic fasting, the most potent natural healing force built into the fabric of our body sanctuary.

This divine healing power is activated when food is limited for a while by using our willpower. Fasting is the unleashing of the doctor of doctors built into the system of all people and animals.

The unique purifying magical sacred fire of a fast ignites in our bodies that powerful energy to cast out all demons and heal many physical, emotional, and mental problems known to man and has been a purification ritual used by people to cure diseases for thousands of years. Unfortunately, fasting is not a widespread method of healing in relation to the rejuvenating of the body. Nevertheless, it is practiced by people who have been fortunate enough to come into the awareness of how to take charge of their health and healing, and in so doing, start to recognize that: **The Body Heals Itself!**

All we have to do is set the right conditions by periodic fasting! The masses seldom use fasting because we have been conditioned to believe that we can't go without food or water for extended periods without starving to death. Nothing could be farther from the truth! Not only can a person go for days without food, but people have been known to go weeks and months without food under the proper supervision. Fasting is the ultimate method to rejuvenate, revitalize, restore the body, and mind to optimal health, and most importantly establishing connection with the Glorious Magnificent Presence!

Chapter Five

Thoughts on Fasting

Because most people have been living on a SAD(Standard American diet) for years it is better to approach a fast in stages. It should be a two-pronged approach. Giving attention to not eating for a while and, at the same time, cleaning out the colon with enemas or colonics. Because a standard western diet has very little natural water content, it is not eliminated quickly from the body, and over time, clogs up all avenues of elimination, such as the intestines, blood vessels, arteries, and the brain.

In America many people suffer from constipation of the whole system because of poor elimination caused by the eating of processed and devitalized foods. A good habit is to eat alkaline foods, such as fresh fruits and vegetables. Fruits and vegetables allow the body to remove waste from the body quickly instead of clogging up the body with constipating foods which take days to digest and eliminate from the body.

Water fasting is a great way to detox the body and should be approached gradually in small increments. An excellent way to start is 24-hour water fast and progressively work up to 7 days with daily enemas.

When a person stops eating during a fast, they no longer have peristaltic action, so taking enemas can help to remove waste safely from the body while fasting. During a fast, when you start to feel miserable, it's only because of the accumulated debris in the system. The problem is that many people have too much waste in their bodies to eliminate from the system through normal avenues of elimination without causing a shock to the system that can create significant discomfort, which may cause many first-time fasters to give up on the fast. Cleaning the bowels is extremely important during a fast, especially if you are new to fasting.

There are four important components/spirits that work together during a fast to make it much more effective: water, air, earth, and the sun.
All of these natural elements (The ancients called them spirits) and spirits work together to effectively and successfully remove toxic waste, expel the devil /parasites and worms from the system through the skin, mouth, nose, etc.

The diseases that are poisoning our reasoning and distorting our sense of reality originate in the colon of humans. Because we are murdering the animals that we eat, consuming the milk that was meant to be consumed by their species, and also eating incompatible combinations of meat, cheese, eggs, that cause premature aging, a lack of energy and decreasing mental clarity

Many of our unhealthy eating habits are handed down to us from our so-called civilized society, and as a result of eating this way, harmful conditions are created in the body. This toxic food does not pass through and exit the body fast enough. It gets compacted in the intestines leaving a film or coating on the intestinal walls of the colon that, over time, turns into mucus and pus, then gets reabsorbed back into the body, poisoning the blood and creating a disease condition all through the body temple. This constipation/compaction sets the stage and condition for parasites and worms (serpents-demons) to fester and build nests in the intestines and from there, migrate throughout the system, causing many diseased conditions and also so-called Cancer.

There is no such thing as Cancer! They created the word and conceptual theory to justify a reason to make more money for the medical society. All diseases are different stages of the same thing. So-called Cancer is just the body telling us that we must radically change our diets and lifestyle practices or face its early dissolution. Even though when a person is born or dies, it's all in the divine plan for the experience of the soul in incarnation.

For those who want to know, true healing is much simpler than we realize and what we have been told. We have been conditioned and educated to become victims of fancy words and machines that take our power and enslave us, dependent on people who don't know how to heal their bodies or anybody! But self-healing is becoming mainstream nowadays, a new day is dawning, and many people are discovering the real cause of disease and how to heal themselves by periodic fasting!

Chapter Six

What is this body

According to science; if we were to use a microscope to take a closer look at the body, the microscope would reveal to us; that what our eyes see and interpret as skin, bone, and flesh is not what it appears to be. On closer look, we can see that, instead of being solid, the body is composed of countless tiny cells, molecules, electrons, photons, neutrons, and atoms that are grouped so close together that they give the body the appearance of being solid. Not only is the body not solid, but all cells, atoms, molecules, electrons, and neutrons, are lifeforms.

These live beings are what give shape to the mental vibrational light energy, which is thoughts. These thought and light energy vibrations are what forms are made of and materialize into the reality of all so-called physical plane forms. The physical world as we know it is only a theory and concept of truth, but on closer observation, it has no basis in actual reality.

Everything is happening within the mind, and all thought forms we misperceive as reality are happening within the mind and are what we witness happening daily. Becoming consciously aware of conditions in the world is a badge and symbol affirming the truth that the world and momentarily life as we see it in our waking days, and nights of sleep, is happening within the domain of the mind's world of mental imaginings.

A world composed of temporary forms that move and take shape, materialize, dissolve, vanish and reappear, and collectively appear within the happenings of our days. These moment-to-moment inaccuracies are happenings and are being played upon the screen of the mind's thought atmosphere. We live in a world of thought, a temporary world of illusionary forms, in this unconscious and unaware dream world of unreality.

Let me explain; The human body and all things in the physical universe are not solid; they just appear that way to the human eye. Many ancient civilizations realized that everything is made out of smaller particles, lifeforms, or spirits of the essence of the thoughtforms vibrational energy created by the mind's continuous and unlimited imaginings, which are materializing and animating forms, altering, and constantly controlling and influencing the lives of people in our world.

Science viewed these particles using their instruments of technology and, depending on their stage or level of introspection, will determine what they see. At this phase of their development, they can perceive and comprehend only matter in their inquiry into the nature of forms.

The spirit of the lifeforms hidden within all things escapes the observation of their limited knowledge as they gaze at the shrouds, which are the shell of the life of the spirit. Using scientific mechanistic instruments to observe physical matter impedes their natural powers of perception and limits their view, to only the outer limits of the boundaries of the essence of the true nature of the mental illusionary form world conception!

Therefore, depending on how far science can advance along the road of progression in the technological development of their instruments of observation will be their ability to see the reality of self-hidden from their view, concealed within the essence of all forms.

One of science's major preoccupations is that wherever and whenever discoveries are made, they should be factual in their analogies, investigations, and findings, which is an excellent standard of quality control that confirms the authenticity of an observation.

It's also an excellent tool to enhance awareness and aid in discovering the endless, infinite variety of forms and physical shapes that materialize in the periphery of their view all because of their insatiable urge to discover and investigate the secrets of the universe and the reality of physical plane matter. Unfortunately, this method of inquiry still doesn't penetrate to the depth of understanding necessary to uncover the hidden self within all things seen. At this stage of our journey, we see that economics appears to be the driving force behind most discoveries.

Scientists are all too often only interested in discovering and learning exclusively about infinite imaginary forms of matter, but some are taking steps in the right direction of revealing the reality of the light of the spirit concealed within all degrees and states of matter. They want to see tangible forms that can be observed and verified by sight and, therefore, can't see life behind all conditions; they can see the live beings concealed in various forms of energy, which make them appear to be solid to the human eye. But in reality, the human eye, by design, was created to interpret the vibrational light energy of the thought forms created by the mind's limited intelligence.

As scientists looked and penetrated deeper into matter, they discovered forms within forms into infinity. Every time they penetrated a state, another form would reveal itself, and the conditions would get smaller, finer and finer. The matter would get so subtle it gradually transforms itself from vibration to energy. For quite some time, this method of inquiry was common practice in the scientific community's preoccupation with the secrets and discoveries of matter, but behind all their scientific groping, in the mysterious depths of the dungeon of their hearts, there is a unquestionable desire to understand the reality of life hidden within all material forms of existence!

The ancients have always known that matter is vibration, vibration is energy, and energy is also thought. The ability of the mind to create thought forms is the result of the mind's imagination, which is limited in its ability to comprehend life factually, therefore It fabricates human reality inaccurately.

This fabrication is false because the images the mind creates are only illusions, seemingly tangible forms that the human eyes perceive that appear to be real, but this perception is wrong because it is interpreted by the restrictions imposed by mundane sense perceptions which are the five senses: sight, touch, hearing, smell, and taste.

The human eyes can only see the illusionary false appearance of forms. If the eyes could see our world instead of the mind's misinterpretations and misperceptions of reality, our world would be seen vastly different, because our world is a world of vibrational, energy, which is thought! The mind is the great creator and distorter of reality behind all appearances.

Everything is happening within your mind, and the mind creates the appearances of the seemingly real, physical world, daily dream reality. But the truth is, the physical plane does not exist and has no factual bases in our false ideas about the world as the physical eyes perceive it. Consciousness your authentic self-dwells beyond the realms of the mind's ability to create illusionary forms, which see everything as being separate from itself. Actually, in reality, there is no separation of things. These perceptions are caused by the mind's distortion of truth, creating the illusion of separate objects and things in the perceived physical world.

You are the conscious and Glorious Magnificent Presence within all things seen, the divine life, which is the consciousness of all living beings. Everything is connected; even inanimate objects have a collective unified spiritual consciousness.

Close your eyes and your ears. Listen to your inner self, listen to the sounds of the world around you, listen to the sound of people talking, listen to your heart beating, listen to the sound of the birds singing, listen to the rustle of the leaves of the trees when the wind is blowing, listen to the sound of the rhythm of your heart beating, listen to the cadence of the melody of the words I am expressing to you, listen! Listen to the sound of the silence of your soul as it beacons you to bask in the joy, peace, love and the melody of the beautiful song of the Glorious Magnificent Presence, as it sings to you in the silence letting you feel and know that it's the Omni Radiant Presence within all things and beings!

If you practice this meditation, you will realize everything is happening inside the consciousness!

If you don't open up your eyes again or go to sleep and do not wake up anymore/experience so-called death, what happens to your world? It disappears. The nature of human reality is inside the human mind's ability to create forms that hide the inner life which is revealed connected within you through meditation. There is an old saying; "The mind is the great slayer of the real!"

Until humans reach the point where they desire peace and the elimination of suffering, advancing to the point in our lives where we finally decide to be the best we can be in thought, word, and deed. We will continue to linger in a deep state of illusion, never going beyond the bondage of the merry-go-round of suffering, trapped within a hamster cage-like wheel of life! Running around and around repeating the same actions that cause the same adverse effects, people will continue to be confined to misery and suffering due to their thinking. Till people start paying attention to their thoughts, they will invariably suffer the consequences of run-away negative thoughts and creating actions without the awareness of the effects which can eventually lead to pain for themselves and others in our temporary short, so-called, material world, life experience.

One day people will realize that their present life circumstances are a direct result of how they think and act in the world. Our thoughts and conduct which develops our present character result from our thinking that determines and weaves the fabric of our present and future reality of circumstances and situations in this mental form world, illusionary reality. Also, how we live in the world determines our current and upcoming life happenings through our conduct and mental day-to-day, moment-to-moment life choices. Our life options are the result of our thinking which is the foundation of the world's suffering.

The world that we find ourselves conscious of is created by thoughts and actions of humans. These thoughts originate from the human mind's creative imagining powers. The energy and vibrations of the mind allow it to have incredibly creative imaginative capabilities. Therefore, on closer observation, we become aware that the foundation of all things seen within the consciousness of the self is the Glorious Magnificent Presence, which is your inner self, the consciousness of all living things!

God did not create the human perception of reality, humans did! If there is a god, you can be assured that God would have better things to do than to create petty human, illusionary realities that is the foundation of much of the suffering that we are experiencing today in our lives. Even though we often attribute our human facts to god's truth, we don't have the slightest clue about understanding God, and all we perceive is what comes out of our present state of mental bondage and ignorance. I recommend doing meditation, and if we do, at the least, we will better understand how we are all connected and how love is the power that will change the world!

When we perceive the body using only our eyes, we fail to see the countless lifeforms, which are all working together, seemingly as though they are working with one mind, to give the body its shape and appearance as it continues to develop, in its various growth stages in life.

What is this invisible force that scientists can't see connecting all these cells and atoms? When we observe things using the intelligence of the mind, we see only illusion and not the actual reality of the images our eyes are showing us in our daily waking consciousness.

A good analogy is Starlings. Sometimes, when a flock of Starlings feels threatened, they can create a pattern with their combined bodies of the illusion of a large bird. Large groups of perhaps hundreds of birds collectively form this image instantly! They use a unity of thought or telepathy to work as one to create the appearance of a large bird to deter unwanted predators.

Imagine a large flock of Starlings occasionally seen flying, often in vast numbers. Sometimes thousands of birds can be observed forming into one large group that scientists call a Murmuration.

If you watch this incredible phenomenon, the birds can instantly change directions like one bird. It's as though one life communicates, manifests, and controls all of the birds simultaneously.

One consciousness appears to be propelling them forward in unison, as though they are one bird with one mind. What an excellent demonstration of how Starlings telepathically communicate in unison showing incredible synchronization without colliding with each other as they fly, especially when trying to evade birds of prey, such as peregrine falcons or sparrow hawks.

And just like thousands of Starlings work together, changing into many shapes and creating many patterns with their collective bodies instantaneously as though they are one mind, so does the mind materialize thoughts made of vibrational thought energy to create the forms, things, and scenes of life that we witness and experience, in the conditions we encounter in our inner thought dream world reality.

There is only one mind and it is the creator and originator of all the forms in the illusion of our momentary dream unconscious experience, which man perceives in his present state of un-awareness, because we live in an inner, mental, dream world reality, an illusionary life created by the mind's mental imaginings.

Chapter Seven

The human eye

Modern scientists use the physical eye and machines to verify the results of their scientific research in many different fields of research. From larger than life forms in nature to small microscopic organisms beyond the range of the observation of the physical eyes. They use the physical eyes as a basis for knowing and observing shapes and forms in life's infinite discoveries.

The human eye is a remarkable powerful organ that man uses to see, investigate, and discover the seemingly real world that he has awakened to find himself in, but the problem is that people have discovered that the eye is limited in its ability to see life as it truly is. Humans are progressively learning what ancients have always known (Consciousness determines what the eyes can see.) The thoughts of the mind can limit and interfere with what the physical eyes see and observe in our daily waking consciousness.

Scientists and the world at large are conditioned to look and search the material forms of the physical universe, to find information and solutions that continue to evade their inquisitive inquiries about the mysteries of how things work, and also the revelation of what things are. It's unimaginable how much money is made on the countless number of material things that are created and manufactured, every second of every day.

Every time scientists look within a form with a microscope, other forms manifest, they see forms, within forms, This amazing phenomenon of never seeing the end of things no matter how far a person looks, and no matter how powerful microscopes and telescopes become, they can only see forms from the mental imaginings of the thoughts of man! Mental cognizant forms are created in the mind of man, not by microscopes or telescopes. Thoughts always precede the manifestation of things,

Everything that man discovers or becomes aware of is born from his imaginative, theoretical perception of reality, and using physical eyesight as his primary means of observation has limited his ability to only see life at the so-called physical level of awareness. But his perception can be enhanced by the discipline of spiritual practices such as concentration and meditation.

The number of forms created by the mind's mental imagining is infinite, it's insatiable appetite to create forms of illusion will go on forever until the birth of the realization, that physical forms and all kinds of matter, whatever the size, shape, or configuration, are just the cover or shell of the one life, which is the absolute being behind all things seen.

Many people from the present, as well as the past, have discovered that the eye is limited in its ability to see life as it truly is, this truth has been tested and understood for centuries, and even now humans are still progressively learning what the ancients have always known, that the eyes are limited in its ability to see life as it is. Someday intuitive perception, clairvoyance, telepathy, and other dormant, undeveloped, and unrealized faculty will be manifested by people who have embarked on the journey of using the will to master the body, emotions, and mind to discover the hidden self within all!

Inside all forms in our unconscious world reality is an intelligence that expresses itself through all life and is beyond the realms of the awareness of man in his current stage of development, using his present mechanistic and mechanical methods of inquiry. Not only is this method of inquiry a problem, but it also limits and impacts his judgments in the way he conducts inquiries. We lean too heavily on mechanical and artificial methods of inquiry not realizing that relying on machine-driven means of examining physical plane phenomena weakens the natural ability to realize the underlying causes of all things. Being too overconfident and comfortable not realizing, or even bothering to mustering up the ambition, to awaken from our somnambulism.

One thing that is certain, the eye is insufficient in its ability to reveal to us what lies behind all forms. The eyes can't see life as it is, and one of the biggest delusions and misperceptions about this surface method of inquiry; is the belief that the only reality is physical, and that authenticity has to be verified by the observation and investigation of the physical world depending on the seeing ability of the human eye to channel information to the brain.

Questioning, investigating, and also observing physical information guided by the human eye is a lucrative monetary preoccupation, and over the years scientists have become addicted to the power of their; continuously developing machines and other synthetic methods of scientific investigations and inquiries, that has resulted in a plethora of inventions and gadgets. They see only the limited perspective that their telescopes and microscopes reveal, which is an artificial theoretical view of the world which is imagined by the miscalculations, and misinterpretations using the mental intelligence of men!

Some people require a moderate pace and other people may take a more rapid approach to self-development, but with just a little bit of conscious effort, and a few simple steps in the direction of positivity and love, we begin to embrace the lifestyle changes necessary to uncloud our vision, transform our personalities and characters, to reflect the beauty that we have inside; it will also allow us to see life as it truly is, beyond the range of the physical eye, to see the magnificent beauty that is hidden behind the cloak and veil of illusion, which hides the soul of material form appearances.

Our world as we see it is changing, and many people are going through the subjective mental process necessary to experience the rebirth of the spirit of consciousness, within their hearts and minds. People are growing more aware, and a deep irresistible, irreversible feeling and desire for peace and love is starting to be felt in the hearts, minds, and souls of people all over the earth.

There is a birth of consciousness happening within people that is increasing a desire in the thoughts and minds of the masses all around the world to embrace the quality of love, which expands our understanding of each other and unites the subjective collective consciousness within all hearts and minds, awakening and imperceptibly kindling the spirit of the life within, prodding us forward to take the necessary steps in our thoughts and actions to make love and peace a reality in the world.

This tantalizing feeling that is stirring so deep within us is often undetected by our conscious mind but is touching the depths of our feelings with such intensity that we are unknowingly experiencing a powerful grand and monumental transition, that is the beginning of the rapture of our lives and is the foundation of the rebirth of our spirit.

Even though some people are content to live sleep walking, traveling through life unaware and deaf to the call and urging of the spirit, even not wanting, or feeling the need, to make the positive steps in establishing the birthing of the god within us. But many of us are starting this necessary process in the manifestation of spirit into life, we are becoming increasingly aware of an intensity of feeling and thought, that it is sending a deep thrill with such a compelling vibrational force of energy, that it is penetrating to the essence of our soul, all the way down to the depth of our being!

Numerous people have this sensitivity, vision, clear view and innate understanding of the direct knowledge and simple understanding of how to create peace in our world, we are beginning to understand that this is a simple, normal, and necessary stage in our development as we go through the process of life in this seemingly real, short, temporary, so-called material, and physical experience, but in reality, is just a mental dream world existence!

Getting to know and understand people through peace and goodwill is the magic formula that will clear our vision to see life as it truly is. This all-inclusive knowledge, wisdom, and understanding will give birth to the feeling and perception of the value of making the power of love a total necessity in our lives and will be at the forefront of our minds and eventually valued beyond measure.

We are coming to a point in our lives where we are comprehending the significance and value of the importance of applying peace and love in our daily interactions with each other. When that day dawns in the morning of the sunshine of our mind, peace, and love will take center stage in all our sincere efforts, and it will become necessary in our relationship with our fellow human beings and Nature.

Chapter Eight

Thoughts and actions

M ost of us doesn't know who we are. It's my opinion that it is very beneficial for people, everywhere, no matter who you are, to leave a little room in your lives for self-improvement.

The more we improve ourselves, making it a priority to pay attention to how we think and act in the world with each other, the better the world becomes.

When we observe the world today, we notice that it appears to be in a deplorable state of mental, moral, and spiritual degradation. This life that we find ourselves in can be significantly changed for the better if we would look in the mirror and see the magnificent beauty and greatness in ourselves. If we take a serious look we will catch a momentary glimpse of the beauty of our inner true nature, our magnificent presence will captivate us and we will gradually or sometimes immediately decide to start the process of elevating and improving our lives, taking the personal responsibility of changing our thoughts and actions according to that image of radiant light and beauty that we see reflected within ourselves and the self of so called others.

Take a deep look! And in so doing, as you inquire from the heart, you will begin to delve deeper into the knowledge and understanding of the wisdom of your soul, and you will start to recognize the love and light of the divine presence in everyone. It's good to take that look, but I believe it is even better to reflect that holy spirit into the world and get into the habit and daily practice of sharing the best parts of ourselves, our love, and compassion with each other!

All human unenlightened thoughts and ideas are like the dark clouds on a stormy day that blocks the radiant light of the sun of the self in all! Hold fast and persevere with your lofty peaceful, and loving thoughts, and you won't backslide, and if you do falter in your honest and consistent effort; the consequences of your actions will be disappointing and emotionally painful that you will be prodded into alignment with your higher self, which has always been there waiting patiently to lovingly guide you back to a state of peace, love, and joy of the glorious light and life of your divine self, which is the essence, energy, and life of all the things you are witnessing in your short mental, illusionary, inner dream world experience.

Most of the time, it takes a dedicated and consistent effort to raise the vibratory rate of our daily thought projection into reality. As we practice this soul-induced method, we began to see the world as it is. We develop this uncommon mental power by training the Mind to think loving thoughts in our daily waking consciousness.

This constant mindful practice will gradually strengthen and increase our ability to maintain a peaceful state of mind by patiently and consistently practicing love and peace in the world, regardless of what life throws our way, It will also enable us to be a silent beacon of light subjectively influencing other souls who come within the radiance of our presence.

As we successfully accomplish and expand to a higher level of spiritual awareness, we will gradually develop a peaceful, calming presence, cultivated and nurtured after many years of self-discipline, by paying attention to the type of thoughts we think daily, and being consistent in our effort to be loving and peaceful in our daily waking consciousness. Over a period of time we will finally radiate this powerful vibrational energy without any conscious effort.

The ancients called this process; The Science of Mind. To accomplish this, one has to be able to feel and see the difference after being out of tune, then getting into alignment with ourselves and nature.

We are spiritual beings in essence but still live under the illusion that the body and its attachments are who we are. I have never been content with the monotony of living a mundane, mediocre lifestyle, I have always loved the challenge of discovering the highest physical, mental, and spiritual capabilities. Some people are born to follow the herd, and some of us are required and have chosen to walk the spiritual path. I respect all directions, love, and recognize the essence and sometimes not too obvious beauty of the spirit in all people.

When people apply love and understanding to their life's circumstances, they will develop the faculty to perceive the real person and not just the body of another being, and a significant reward of that process is, it gives a person the ability to see themselves in others.

Hence the old saying; Do unto others as you would want them to do to you. If we saw other people and animals like ourselves. It would definitely hasten the process of creating peace in the world. The power and energy of the consistent practice and application of love will create joy in ourselves, also the energy of our love will certainly influence others. Expressing this loving vibrational energy from the soul will transform our world beyond conflict and discord into a world of joy, happiness, and peace.

When we use the magical process of thinking loving thoughts a living light of consciousness, an intuitive light that will illuminate our path, assisting us silently, quietly weaving our positive dreams into reality. And like a spider weaves its web, we will also learn how to use intuition and love as a tool in our life to shape our destiny, and that power can, and will, shape, unfold, and manifest in our life according to the results of our thinking.

This fantastic daily, hour, minute, and second ritualistic mindfulness is a beautiful self-discipline that works wonders if we are sincere in our efforts. When a person applies this method of thinking their thoughts will be changed to a higher vibrational frequency, intuitively and unconsciously influencing the thoughts of others with the radiating and transformational power of their habitual positive, loving, and peaceful thought vibrational energy.

As you continue to apply this self-discipline to your life, you will become more aware of how to heal yourself and others from physical, emotional, and mental disorders. Your life will be more meaningful with a greater sense of purpose and direction and you will experience an increased love and understanding of life.

Also, because of your daily thought practices, you will develop peace in your heart, love in your Mind, and joy in your soul, regardless of the situational occurrences you encounter in your day.

No matter what comes your way, you will not be moved from being persistent and maintaining a perpetual balance as you begin to use your will to develop your indomitable ability, and natural habit of thinking peaceful, powerful, joyful, and loving thoughts, twenty-four hours a day. And no! You will not ever be bored! On the contrary, you will begin to realize that you are on the ancient sacred, mystical, and magical journey down the spiritual path of life, initiating an odyssey, a profound experience, an incredible thrill, and joy, of the deep satisfying delight of being at one with yourself and others.

As you travel through life in this world that is happening within you, you will begin to recognize that everything and everyone is woven out of the Mind's imaginings, thought energy vibrations, which are lifeforms. These lifeforms all work together as one Mind to give our thought world reality its shape and form. The Mind creates these forms that are your seconds, minutes, hours, days, and moments in your day-to-day dream world reality.

.

The Mind is the master of making illusionary images from immeasurable numbers of vibrations and energy. It creates the illusion of life's mental and imaginary moments throughout our day. These particles of thought, which appear to be matter, vibration, and energy, are live-conscious lifeforms. These beings or lifeforms are the thought forms of vibrational thought energy images of the Mind's creative imaginings.

These imagined particles are one of the Mind's primary attributes, and it constantly creates and imagines these forms that appear on the screen of our mental cognition. The sounds, shapes, and images created by the Mind's creativity and the moments and experiences of our imagined life in physical plane existence are happening within the world of the Mind's thought reality. The Mind's ability to create thought forms by thinking them into reality is the basis and foundation of life's misperceived, temporary existence in the unreality of our collective brief, physical, form life, and inner thought world experience.

If you are experiencing or witnessing a day in this life, at some point in your consciousness development, you may become aware of the observation point beyond mental imagining. This point of reference will allow your soul to witness the tremendous power of the creative Mind and how it weaves the fabric of our temporary existence in this inner thought, dream world reality.

What I am talking about and describing is a well-kept secret buried deep within all hearts, readily available and reserved for those spiritual aspirants who have felt or are in the process of hearing the irresistible call and beaconing of the spirit, the faint whispering of the self-calling your soul back to its magnificent, illuminating, and illustrious brilliance. And finally, once again, to bask in the full glory and realization of who you are as you stand in full recognition and awareness of the radiance of the Glorious Magnificent Presence! The wonderous life within all things!

The Mind creates form in the world as it attempts to manifest life through its robust, deceptive imagining and image-making ability. The momentary scenes of life dissolve and disappear over time, and like fog dissipating on a damp morning before the appearance of the radiating bright light of the sun. And just like the fog, depending on its density can create a veil concealing actual reality behind itself, so does the body conceal the radiant light and life of the spirit within itself. Depending on the depth and thickness of your Mind's ignorance will be your ability to penetrate through the haze in the Mind to perceive the reality of the one life behind all forms of life.

Chapter Nine

The Ultimate Journey

Ultimately Sometimes, someday, in some life, your mind will feel the promptings and urge of the spirit, an irresistible silent call beckoning it to listen and redirect its attention from its preoccupations with images created within itself. When this happens, the mind will eventually change the course of its actions of unlimited, perpetual weaving of illusionary forms of thought vibrational energy.

Afterwards as the Mind pauses to listen, it is captivated by the calming spell and magnetic attraction of the spirit as it turns to gaze in the direction of the brilliant light of the sun of the Magnificent Glorious Presence. And once the Mind redirects its gaze and observes the luminosity and bright light of the of the Glorious Magnificent Presence, it will be humbled into complete silence, captivated by the magic of the omnipresent rays as it gradually establishes a bridge or link between the mind and the divine self.

When the self establishes a link with the mind, the mind listens more to the divine self. It ceases to be as self-absorbed, totally preoccupied with its own illusionary, imaginary creative misperceptions. When the spirit beckons, the mind begins to do more listening instead of fabricating and creating temporary illusions in a multiplicity of thought forms. It starts to pay more attention to what constitutes actual reality in life, and slowly and occasionally rapidly, it develops the faculty and mental capacity to focus on a new quest. A quest to find the way by paying attention to the inner urge of the soul's prompting as the mind seeks to discover the reality behind all things seen.

This transformation will significantly enhance your life. You will enthusiastically look forward to taking advantage of every opportunity to express thoughts and actions with genuine compassion and heartfelt love for others. As you develop this vision, you will perceive and know the reality of the Glorious Magnificent Presence within all forms. You will finally get a glimpse of whom you are in relation to others in this temporary mental, intellectual dream world reality as you progressively raise your awareness of the identity of the authentic self-concealed behind the scene of the forms of all beings.

As you progress along this path of love, you will get into the rhythm and habit of creating loving thought vibrations in your mind, and you will also learn how to persevere in your actions; to purposely and consistently apply this quality of thought energy more and more frequently in your daily life's reality; and as a spider weaves its web, you will also begin to weave the web of the fabric of your everyday life reality. By cultivating peaceful, powerful, and loving thoughts, your perception of the existence of world happenings will change.

Because thoughts are things, and as you Row, Row, Row your boat gently down the stream of life, you will realize that; Merrily, Merrily, Merrily, Merrily, Life is but a dream!

This words of this song innocently reveals the truth about life and shares profound wisdom about how we should live our lives to experience less strife and discord, and as a result of this high and noble thought process, you will discover the most unique, powerful being hidden within all things seen. **The Glorious Magnificent Presence!**

Chapter Ten

The transformational power of
Concentration and Meditation

Meditation is an excellent method to start the process of spiritual growth and awareness because it quiets the surface chatter of the mind which enables us to develop the habit of noticing and paying attention to the preoccupations and distractions of the type and quality of thoughts that randomly surface in the mind's mental atmosphere. Arbitrary Thoughts that appear in our awareness stop the mind from interpreting reality accurately. We begin to notice that these thoughts are a continuous, reoccurring, habitual distraction, keeping us from seeing the fact of life.

As we begin to practice Meditation consistently, we will start to notice that thoughts which come into our minds are repetitive and often appear in our awareness without any effort, seemingly without any rhyme or reason. These thoughts that appear in our mind all too often are not even our thoughts but have been repeatedly programmed into our minds by society, parents' friends, media, etc. As we become more consistent in our practice, we realize that some people are not very successful in meditation because of their inability to focus and concentrate.

Learning how to concentrate by focusing our mind on a subject or object for a while using willpower is a significant prerequisite to actually successfully practicing Meditation. For Meditation to be effective in the preliminary stages of one's practice, one should develop the ability to observe the continuous stream of thoughts that surface in the atmosphere of the mind. Meditation requires paying attention to our thoughts initially, and then not stopping the stream of thoughts, but instead, no longer noticing the thoughts of the mind until they are no longer happening within our awareness! Many of us lack the concentration necessary to take advantage of this unique quality without getting distracted by the pageantry and parade of thoughts coming and going in the atmosphere of the mind. Observing and noticing one's thoughts is essential to cultivating a good meditation posture.

Also, concentration when mastered will enable a person to retain lessons learned from meditation, such as bringing the fruits of our meditation into our daily thought and lifestyle practices. Concentration enables us to notice random thoughts that surface in our mind creating a distraction that interferes with our ability to focus, and the culmination of our ability to focus and concentrate will initiate the process of the cessation and dissolution of thought!

Habitual random thoughts are nothing new; just regurgitated thoughts passed on from mind to mind, parroted robotically by many people who rarely have any experience using the practical application or the self-discipline they claim to have followed to come to their present state of unawareness. This quality of thought passed on to us by culture forms our current character shaped by the preconceived notions, suggestions, and assumptions of others. This mental conditioning binds us to a cycle of thoughts that is a mental prison that stymies and retards our progression in our self-development.

Of course, I have realized that many people are comfortable and feel a sense of comfort knowing that they are living a so-called everyday life and have no desire to do anything else. They do not realize that we are confined in a prison of thought, locking us within someone else's perception of reality. Meditation develops the faculty and ability to transcend and slowly awaken from our unconscious somnambulate state of unawareness and frees us from the influence of the thoughts and opinions of others. Especially unsubstantiated beliefs and experiences that we have no prior knowledge or experience.

Meditation teaches us how to shape and mold our world according to how we think in the world; By learning how to use the power of thought mindfully and responsibly, we become masters of our own destiny.

Modern day humanity is still interpreting reality through the mind body experience within the limited perception of the faculty of the mind's mental imaginings! The perception of subjects, objects and any forms are an illusion of a mind that has not been mastered and still not basking in the radiance of the divine presence. The mind is the creator of all happenings which only exist within the mind's mental imaginings. We live an imagined reality arranged within the mind of all, which is an inner thought world reality.

There are no outer spaces, on the contrary, everything is happening within. We will discover the truth when we personally walk the path of enlightenment instead of following various souls that fumble along the path and prison of the mind's mental intellectual ignorance. Very few aspirants can give us an accurate description to take us beyond the pitfalls and snares of delusions. Unless you personally experience the journey yourself, you may not see the error of their misinterpretations, often carried over, parroted and shared from man to man for centuries as they endeavor to pierce the vail without the mastery of self, to no avail, living in the imagined limited awareness of the minds mental jail, which is a hindrance to basking in the radiance of the wonderful, brilliant, luminosity of the **Glorious Magnificent Presence!**

The study and understanding of European cosmos conception don't indicate or validate the true interpretation of the vibration and energy of the soul. Self-discipline allows us to personally take the journey beyond the boundary of Eurocentric speculation and theories which is not a true interpretation of a true spiritually experience. If we do take the necessary steps in the process of enlightenment, it is revealed to us just how far the so-called masters have themselves progressed beyond the jail of the boundaries of the minds ignorant, intellectual, illusionary mental speculation!

The problem is, the hallmark of those that don't know the way are those that are constantly seeking a middle way to continue to play and dabble in nonsense, error prone, habitual behavior without any thought of the consequences! Easier way is what they are trying to say. Of course, everyone is on the right track according their life experience. There is only one life in this temporary dream world existence and because of our mental conditioning we see others, differences, cultures locations, countries, girls, boys, cows, dogs, cats and not the essence behind the cloak of forms. Even though we are presently having a great time in our perception, witnessing, and experiencing life's diversity, its bases is the illusion of separation!

Whether it's the mystic or holy men of 10,000 years ago or modern-day man, conceptions and theories change but the process of true enlightenment remains the same. And that process is, in order to escape beyond the bondage of the ignorance of the mind's mental imaginings a seeker of truth much slay the dragons of the lower nature in order to develop the faculty of true enlighten spiritual perception. Self-master is the prerequisite for establishing a connection and communication with the glory of the divine Omni spiritual presence, and also to be a proper vessel to accommodate the intense influx of the vibrational and transformational energy of the highest, which transcends the intellectual babbling of the minds mundane processes of thought!

The process and methods of the way can only be indicated by others as they grope and stumble around in the darkness of their own shortcomings searching for enlightenment by living in shadow of their own soul, hypnotized by the joys and passions of living a temporary ordinary existence of all types of sense gratifications that offer only temporary joys and constant emotional and mental bondage that is a barrier to true enlightenment.

but there are no short cuts to true enlightenment and only the masters know the way, and the mastery, cultivation and use of the will must come into play, using the will power and self-discipline to go beyond the nonsensical, intellectual rhetorical rhythms of a slave to the body! There is only one master in this dream world reality and everyone else is in the process of becoming which, we realize as we personally experience and walk the path of true enlightenment! Not just talking the talk but walking the walk!

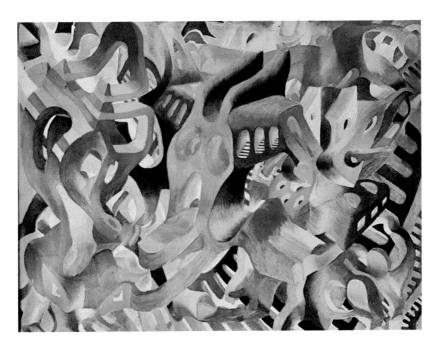

Chapter Eleven

Man's Unlimited Realms of

Possibilities

I realize and hope that in writing this book and by sharing this information, you, Dear reader, will understand and know that what I share with you is the result of me making necessary sacrifices in my life's experiences to phantom the depths of my heart, rise to the level of self-confidence and courage of spirit to share with you through this book, the results of my life long journey of traveling within, exploring my soul to discover the meaning and purpose of human life, in the imaginary form world, and mental conception of reality.

As I make such bold thoughts available in these writings, I am not under the illusion that what I am revealing will be understood or excepted by the masses, and collectively we may never see the same vision of life. But I know of a certainty that; someday, in some period of your growth, you may get to a stage in your life's journey where you come to realize; If you practice paying attention to how you think in the world, and also taking the time to think peaceful and loving thoughts in your day. Also, if you establish the mindful discipline and habit of paying attention to how you think, the world will be changed for the better.

If you start his mindful self-discipline, and practice this consistently, you will notice a change in your attitude, conduct, and activities in your day; after a while, you will begin to see the positive results of your consistency, and if you make these changes in your thoughts a habit, you will become more successful in using your willpower to initiate and practice, healthier lifestyle choices. You will also begin creating a genuine, consistent, practice of using love in your daily life that will eventually result in dreams, thoughts, desires, and feelings that will inspire you to continue to follow the direction of the liberation of your soul, from the bondage of ignorance, by the guidance of the spirit, of the ever-present luminosity, of **The Glorious Magnificent Presence!**

As a result of this effort, you will transform your thought atmosphere and subjectively change the world around you. The sincerity of your love will influence everything that comes into the aura and radiance of your presence. The more you practice love, the more dynamic and powerful its energy will become in its manifestation to bring about change in your world.

You have within you the ability to use the power of love like a broom to sweep your mind free of negative thoughts. Using love in your thoughts and actions transforms your mind into a dynamic force for change, enabling you to create powerful thought vibrations of peace within yourself; you will become a beacon of positivity to the world, radiating your positive vibrational thought energy subjectively into the mind of others without any conscious effort on your part, what so ever.

Someday in the not-too-distant future, people will start exhibiting feats that we thought were only true in fairy tales because the effects of consciously thinking peaceful and loving potent thoughts can change the frequency of your mind and unleash the power to help transform the minds of others, in the collective spirit of all. Then the consciousness of the world in all beings will change the world into a garden of Eden. And yes, I'm just a dreamer, but I'm not the only one!

Chapter Twelve

Children of the future

Let's talk about children. A good analogy is; When we buy a new car, we must put good gas in it for it to operate at its full potential. Also, when we are responsible for raising a child, we should strive to be the best we can be in their presence. When we are in the company of children, we should try to be good role models and examples, knowing they always want us to show them the way.

Our thoughts, words, and deeds are essential to help shape and develop good character in our children and ourselves. Most people would agree, that a sunny radiant disposition is, without a doubt, a valuable asset to anyone's personality. It would be so wonderful if our children could have parents who have come to the realization, as a couple, to agree to work together to develop in themselves good character because they understand the value of applying love and understanding to their lifestyle practices, knowing this can significantly affect the child's disposition, personal character, and conduct in life.

Parents mindfully and positively reshaping their characters will significantly affect, transform and enhance a child's thought and emotional life, which will be balanced with the light of the conscious spirit, which is the fulcrum and axis of good judgment that is a priceless aid to support and guide the child through the many trials and tribulations that they will encounter as they go through life. The conscious self is the tremendously, powerful, and valuable ultimate presence, which is the balancing axis at the core of understanding in the child's mind.

The child's soul can be infused with positivity and love from our example and brought to the forefront of a child's consciousness by the power of the parents' habits and thoughts. The enlightened thoughts of parents can stir and awaken the spirit and intelligence of the conscious self within the child. The self is a guardian light that is always present, always patient, waiting to be a wonderful guide to aid in helping to direct the child's steps along the path of life.

When raising children, we should always care about how we think and act in and out of their presence. As we become good role models to our children in our thoughts and actions, it increases their chances of being happy and successful in the world because we shape their character by our example, which will minimize unnecessary suffering as they go through their trials and tribulations in life.

As they learn how to think using love in their associations and experiences, a transformation occurs within the child's hearts and minds. This change within the child's mind enhances and refines their sensibilities and stimulates the child's capacity to experience and feel empathy, compassion, and love for others. It is beautiful when parents decide to be living, breathing, and walking examples of love.

Someday it will become common practice to see parents who have seen the vision and value of demonstrating love in their actions and reactions to life being consistent in their efforts in every moment. Helping the child to naturally form the habit of gravitating toward and being attracted to genuine, loving thought vibrations with whatever situation life throws their way. This will ensure that a child learns self-control, develops good thought habits, and becomes a force for good in the world.

And yes, love purifies consciousness, and a loving, peaceful mind can eventually cause some people to exhibit miraculous powers. Since space and time are man's perception of reality (imagined by man.)

Since walls are not solid, (of course we think they are) even though a man with his instruments can see through walls. His thoughts and feelings travel through objects, transverse distances in short periods, and defy gravity, which he already does with his planes and drones. The next step is personally defying gravity. These feats are all within man's unlimited realms of possibilities and will manifest periodically as man advances along the path and journey to the realization of the self.

Chapter Thirteen

The life that you are!

would like to start this chapter to remind everyone of how long you have been on this journey and how all human experiences are your experiences because you are the one in all. And as we walk this path, it will appear that some paths lead to discontentment, disease, and conflicts, because everywhere we look, the roads of life seem full of negative impediments of dissatisfaction, disease, and war! And over time, as we begin to see the state of the world, its people, and governments, we start longing and looking for a change.

The most potent force for change in the world is the changing of our consciousness which is the key and source of the whole kaleidoscope of daily, mental, and worldly events, which is a temporary stage but necessary part of our illusionary, mental, imaginary, momentary human existence, this is a journey and process of life which will transform our world into a paradise, which will be the result of how we think in our daily waking dream consciousness.

Because thoughts are things, it is important to pay attention to the type of thinking that we do in our day because these thoughts materialize into the scenes and events we encounter as we travel on the journey through life. As a result of this high and noble process of watching your thoughts, you will discover the most unique, powerful being hidden within all things seen. **The Glorious Magnificent Presence!**

.

When we progressively master the artistic and lofty self-discipline of determining what we will allow our minds to think we will discover that our life will be enhanced and eventually changed for the better. As a result of this practice, we will become more aware of the value of cultivating love in our minds, peace in our hearts, and joy in our souls. We will begin sculpting our thoughts into forms of the spirit that will change the world's reality, starting with ourselves, by using loving and peaceful thoughts whose vibrations will create tranquility in our mind and consciousness until we begin to see and feel the magnificence and beauty of the spirit in all beings.

What amazes and humbles me is to know what happens as a result of someone consciously paying attention to what they will allow themselves to think, When people are mindful of their thoughts their world outlook is changed awakening and enhancing the perception of the senses and achieving much clarity of thought. If we steadfastly, persevere, and consistently develop a daily routine, practicing the ancient magical and mystical thought discipline, of thinking loving, joyous, and peaceful thoughts throughout our life, we will notice a wonderful transformation occurring in our consciousness that changes the way we view and understand life.

As a result of this incredible mental discipline and noteworthy sacrifice, our life can be profoundly changed and transformed in how we see the world in our daily interactions with others. This practice will develop the faculty and spiritual vision in us to recognize the divine life in all.

The life that you are lives concealed behind the scene of your human body and is present, always witnessing and observing your continuous growth and development throughout the various stages of your life. From birth, adolescence, old age, and eventually, so-called death. The real you is the quiet onlooker who is behind the curtain and background of your life, can and will manifest, according to the quality of thoughts that you create in your mind, during your temporary, momentary sojourn in your life of form, in this mental, earth life experience.

According to science, your body is entirely renewed at all stages of growth and development. It also changes every cell and tissue every seven to ten years except for the cells in our brain, heart, and eyes, which are with us our entire lives. (according to scientific theories and limited observation). That's because dissolution and the renewal of cells and atoms are in perpetual motion and transformation throughout our life in this human form, whether or not we can observe the changes that are taking place. After all, the constant condition of change is the nature of forms.

But one thing that does not change in this life is your divine presence which is the real you. The energy of the spirit within that animates and gives your body its purpose and meaning in your so-called physical life, does not change. It is an eternal constant unalterable presence.

The life that you are becomes more conscious and aware by experiencing life's trials and tribulations in this body, and ultimately the experiences gained through progressively learning how to manage thought while we are in this body will help us to create more positive and loving thought forms that will shape and transform our destiny and harmonize our mental experience in the world, and perhaps awaken us to the consciousness and awareness of our authentic self, hidden within and without, in the realms of our, imaginary, dream world existence.

Chapter Fourteen

Thoughts about loved ones
who has passed on?

Am writing this chapter about a subject that I have always wanted to discuss with people I know concerning any loved ones that have recently transitioned beyond this world experience.

The question is this! If you had a chance to bring someone back to life, at what age would you want them to come back to life? At what stage of life would you like for them to come back? Would you like your loved one to return to life at the same age and time they died? Would you want them to come back younger, or would you like them to come back older or the same as when they left?

When we lose someone, we often feel a sense of loss and miss their presence in our lives because we are accustomed to having them around and experiencing their presence in some capacity.

But the truth is, although we experience lots of wonderful, memorable, unique, relationships with friends and loved ones in life, and even though these experiences are by far beyond compare, in actuality, we barely scratch the surface of the complexity of whom they were in essence, only knowing faction of them as a person, other than what they look and feel like to us. I know that this comment will probably rub some people the wrong way but all too often our experience and perception of others is often viewed by how we think and feel about them, depending on our mood, not knowing that the person is in reality, that timeless, changeless being underneath the veil of the egoic personality,

Imagine if you asked a person who had just died at what age they would like to return to if they could have another day in this life. Your friend or loved one would probably not want to reincarnate at the age, or stage of life, that you would like them to, they would probably have a different answer than you.

The previous example shows how attached we are to physical bodies, and not to the soul of the actual spirit the body represents.

The beauty of the spirit's life in the bodies of our loved ones and friends who have departed causes us to have sorrow after they leave their bodies of flesh. But their spirits continue to live on within our minds, and their presence lingers in our hearts, watering our thirst for their continued presence in our lives.

Most of the time even though we may feel that we have experienced and shared the incomparable essence of the people or person who has departed, the truth is, we never get a glimpse or anywhere close to knowing the life of the presence which we chose to love inside the people and animals that passed through and shared our experiences.

Whether they are a lover, a friend, a family member, or pets, we hardly ever get to know the divine spirit that the person's body represents; what we see, feel and experience is just a fragment of the magnificent presence that they and we are.

Periodically we may get a glimpse, but the life that's present within does not reveal its true identity to us, until we live our highest and noblest life in our thought practices, especially practicing love in our daily interactions with others! Afterward, our eyes will be opened to see the light of the divine presence shining through the forms of all things.

Until we begin to live our lives trying to become the best we can be, we will continue to not see life and people in life for who they are, **The Glorious Magnificent Presence!**

By cultivating the practice of paying attention to how we think and live in our world, we remove the ignorant mental barriers and blocks in our hearts and minds which create the illusion that we are different and separate from others. The truth is, there are no others!

There is only one life experiencing life on this mental plane of imaginary existence. This life shines brightly within the form of all things and beings because we are living in a waking dream and experiencing a world where everything is thought.

The forms of life that we are experiencing are all thought forms created by the mind's imaginings. As time goes by, in the not-so-distant future, more and more people will develop the vision to see life and the people in it as they are, not as a physical body, but as beautiful radiant light beings, full of the magnificent beauty of a conscious fully awakened soul.

Even as I speak, the great awakening is taking place within the consciousness of the masses, and this inner subjective urge is subjectively stimulating the spirit within the minds of many people, kindling the fire of their desires to begin the necessary steps, taking full possession of the latent powers that everyone has when they are born into this world.

That power is the ability to create love in our world with the creative power of thought! We will learn to master and use this creative power which is the energy that's necessary for enlightening and transforming our world.

All humans have been gifted with the gift of immortality! Nothing and no one are ever lost on this plane of existence. There is no such thing as death! Live cannot be destroyed by man in his dream world reality.

Man cannot hurt or destroy life, which seemingly inhabits the so-called physical body for a short period in this temporary earth experience. That amazing life is the Glorious Magnificent Presence which is the light and life of all beings plus all things seen, within the domain of the mind's imagining; the world of illusion where most feeble human minds dwell!

HUMANITY HAS fallen from GRACE. And that's why suffering has taken its place; Let us remember we are just passing through this inner thought world reality, on our way home to a greater and broader comprehension of who we are in relation to others, and eventually realizing, **there are no others**!

There is only one life in life, and it shines through and is reflected within the light in everyone's eyes. It is the illuminated path of the light and wisdom that leads to paradise **and the realization that; You are the One in All!**

Chapter 15

Love is that power!

Love is the power that will change the world, and by us applying the daily ritual of thinking loving thoughts, and practicing love and peace in our day, a transformation will take place in our character, hearts, and minds, which will radiate to all who comes into the aura of our presence.

If we want to see the world change for the better, we must use love to change ourselves, especially how we think. We must be sincere in our effort to embrace love and peace in our hearts and minds because that love is contagious; it is the most powerful force and energy in our lives.

By us creating love in our minds first and then spreading and sharing that love in our world, our world and life will be miraculously transformed by our efforts. Our consistent and sincere practice of thinking loving thoughts, practicing and sharing our love in all of our relations and associations with others, will eventually establish the bridge that will connect us with the higher spirit in ourselves and will also transform, kindle, and help to ignite the cosmic fire, the dazzling and unique radiant light, subjectively influencing and stimulating positivity in the soul of others, because we are all connected.

All hearts and minds are connected because there is only one mind; it is the source, beginning,

and end of all forms in this consciousness and
mental dream reality shared equally by all.

Chapter Sixteen

Your Will Power

A lot of people can talk about knowledge but when it comes to applying that knowledge to our daily life, we often fall flat on our faces.

Very few men or women want to use their will power to overcome the obstacles to physical, emotional, mental, and spiritual healing and peace in the world. We can all talk the talk, but can any of us walk the walk?

The internet is a good platform and avenue for false prophets to hide, masquerade, or promote information and knowledge they have with little actual practice and experience. But when it comes time to, indeed, apply this knowledge to our lives, we fail miserably in our weak lackluster efforts, or make lame excuses! I am not trying to convert anyone but just passing on and sharing a personal observation.

For example, if you look at our faces, especially the skin of the face and under the eye. These details can be a great mirror to show us our past sins and, with the proper experience, can tell us precisely the nature and cause of what is creating diseases in our physical, emotional, and mental, bodies.

We are living in a period that offers a opportunity to heal ourselves and the world because nowadays, many people are becoming aware of how to heal the mind and body. At the moment we have a chance to learn how to use the power of the will, which is lying latent within every one of us, to transform things in our nature that are causing us unhappiness, disappointments and disease in our lives. By the way, instead of just focusing on, and complaining about what we see other people doing or experiencing. It's time for us to shine the light of our efforts illuminating the dark recesses of a lack of sufficient determination on our part, to master and elevate ourselves beyond our shortcomings. Let's not be hypocrites! We should practice what we preach!

There's an old saying, everybody wants change, but nobody is willing to change!)
The world is just a reflection of the quality of our thoughts.

Let's be the change that we want to create in the world, by getting up off of our butts, paying better attention to what we think say and do in the world, and always remembering that thoughts are things that always manifest according to how and what we think!

Chapter Seventeen

Conclusion

As I conclude this short book, I want to thank the reader for joining me in my mental inner-world journey exploring the misconceptions of man's transitory limited theoretical understanding about what constitutes the nature of actual reality.

There is something that I want to reiterate of the utmost importance in your quest for self-realization or self-improvement.

In the previous chapters, I addressed the issue and question of what is this so-called outside life experience that we so ignorantly and loudly exclaim and proclaim to be so real other than a fragment of our intellectual lack of self-knowledge.

I explained how nothing on this level of so-called material, intellectual, and mental unconsciousness state of unawareness is real.

We also explored the concept of matter and how all so-called matter is just an illusion and how all forms in this ignorant and unconscious dream-like state of awareness that most feeble minds dwell is matter, and matter does not matter, and is not matter at all!

We also explored how matter is vibration, how vibration is energy, and energy is thought. Through introspection, concentration, and meditation, the ancients realized that everything is mental in our present state of the mind's inner world of mental imaginings. The thought world we perceive in our daily dream world of unaware consciousness misconceptions occurs within the mind's thought atmosphere.

We also discussed the prerequisite to attain a state of awareness that will allow us to see the Magnificent Glorious Presence in all and how to achieve and maintain this quality and stage of self-discipline, and self-mastery that the average seeker of truth is, too often, not ready to follow.

We also discussed the ancient practices necessary to master the body, its sensations, and insatiable cravings for all kinds of wants and endless desires.

One of the most critical topics I discussed in the previous chapters is paying attention to what we think daily, practicing concentration in addition to mindfulness, in the early stages of our spiritual journey as a base and springboard to an effective meditation practice.

Also, something to remember is that the concept of human thought, of or about anything, is dictated by the mind's mental imaginings, which only imagines illusions! The mind's imagined theories of energy, or the make-believe concept of anything, is nothing but puny humans groping in the dark cavern of wild mental human speculation! It's all just the shell of actual reality that can only be grasped if the mind has been mastered, and the emotions and body appetites have been tamed! Very few people attain that level of consciousness and the powerful ability to gaze into the eyes of the sun of the one divine omni Presence! There is no outside world! We live in an inner thought world, an imagined dream reality!

Remember until people progress significantly along the avenue of self-development, they will continue their misinformed journey through the maze of the mind's endless misconceptions about the nature of actual reality, they will also suffer the consequences of their actions which will create pain, suffering, and also the discomfort necessary to change the error and direction of their ways. The spirit behind the scene is always working lovingly, persuading, gently and quietly transforming their lives, turning them in the direction of the brilliant light illuminating the path of right judgment in the basic life lessons which are absolutely necessary to create an inner peace that develops the power of the master mind, a small reflection of the **Glorious Magnificent Presence!**

Thank you so much for joining me on this journey in this small book exploring the timeless, infinite awareness and conscious realization of The **Glorious Magnificent Presence**, which is sought by many but genuinely realized by few.

Respectfully Yours in Peace, Love, Happiness, and Joy,

Monad Elohim Graves

About the Author

Monad Graves Elohim is a multidisciplinary artist that embodies his first name by creating his art with the purpose to become consciously aware of the amazing, beautiful life, concealed within all beings in our daily waking life experience.

Monad has an intense love of nature and a deep appreciation for his worldly life experience walking among the beautiful people of the earth, and he is also thankful for being born in human form because it allows him to demonstrate, practice, and share his thoughts of love, peace, and joy in the world, through the imaginative, creative, and original nature of his sculptures and his personal lifestyle choices.

Monad's art is a symbolical representation of his inner and outer thought practices that he has eagerly shared with people constantly for over 50 years and his work has been fueled by a need to know, a need to learn, and a need to grow more spiritually into the awareness of who he is in relation to everyone else.

He feels a sense of unity and oneness with all nature and has also learned to trust himself by allowing originality and a natural spontaneity to come through in his work, as he goes through the subjective and imaginative mental creative process;

a process that has revealed to him the secret of how to free the soul from the bondage of the mind's mental imaginings and align oneself with The **Glorious Magnificent Presence!**

This book is just a fragment and a small step in the direction of the noble path of that incredibly unique awareness.

Made in the USA
Columbia, SC
24 April 2023

66365ffc-a3d1-4dde-960d-564c11060b0fR01